The Little Book of
Wisdom for Dealing
with Frustration

The Little Book of Wisdom for Dealing with Frustration

Godly Wisdom for Everyday Life

Dr. Adrian Manley

Library of Congress Control Number: 2014909705
ISBN: Hardcover   978-1-4990-2765-5
                 Softcover   978-1-4990-2764-8
                 eBook   978-1-4990-2767-9

Edited by Denise McCabe ~ www.mccabeediting.com
Christ Centered Fellowship Publishers

This book was printed in the United States of America.

Rev. date: 06/19/2014

To order additional copies of this book, contact:
Xlibris LLC
1-888-795-4274
www.Xlibris.com
Orders@Xlibris.com
550456

TABLE OF CONTENTS

GODLY WISDOM FOR EVERYDAY FRUSTRATION

Aggravated	Disappointed	Disturbed	Sick and Tired	Troubled
Agitated	Dismayed	Exasperated	Ticked off	Upset
Angry	Displeased	Heated	Tired	Uneasy
Annoyed	Distraught	Irritated	Tired of being	Vexed
Bothered	Distressed	Perturbed	sick and tired	Worn out

TAKE ANY THREE of these and you have some pretty serious angst going on. But you have probably found yourself experiencing several of these kinds of emotions at one time either ongoing or frequently. Yikes! How's a person to cope? This book gives you 7 assurances from God and more than 50 tips from me to help you deal effectively with the harsh realities of life. In addition, you will be given The 5 Steps for Frustration Transformation Form that will make it easy for you to reduce the frustration in your life.

Specifically maybe

- Your spouse doesn't seem to get the point and continues negative behavior
- Your children are acting out and getting into trouble in school
- You are not making the money you want to make
- Ministry is bringing more challenges than rewards
- Family is a challenge, Work is a challenge, and Church is a challenge

All of these things and more become a source of frustration in the lives of people everywhere. Indeed, many people live every day in an unhealthy emotional state as a result of frustration. I am convinced that the devil strategically endeavors to keep believers (and others) frustrated, stressed, and discouraged. The devil knows that frustrated people are less healthy, less effective, less loving, less motivated, and less at peace with God, themselves, and others. Therefore, the healthy and the right thing to do is to find godly answers for dealing with frustration. God has given you these answers in the Bible.

While it is true that we cannot prevent all frustrating circumstances, in this book you will discover both why you should and how to avoid a good amount of frustration in life. In fact, you will also gain a greater understanding of your frustration and how to actually deal with it so effectively that you can *benefit from it* and be able to *let it go!* Yes, you really can use your frustration and then get rid of it.

Included in this book are many scriptural quotations. Unless otherwise noted, they are from the New International Version (NIV) of the Bible. Other versions used are the New Living Translation (NLT) and the King James Version (KJV).

ACKNOWLEDGMENTS

ABOVE ALL AND first of all I want to acknowledge and thank My Lord and Savior Jesus Christ. HE has been the driving force to make my life what it is today.

I want to thank my amazing wife Katrina for always supporting me through this and every other project.

In addition, there are many others to whom I want to express my deep and heartfelt thanks:

- My two children who inspire me daily
- My loving mom, Terry Davis, who constantly shows her love and support
- My (S)hero and grandmother Ocrietto Anderson who willingly dedicated her life to providing me with a better life than she had
- My sister, Sherry Davis, the world's greatest aunt and babysitter
- My very gifted editor, Denise McCabe, for her amazing ability to shine, polishes, and enhance my writing without compromising the message
- My pastor Dr. Detroit Williams for his mentorship and guidance
- The Christ Centered Fellowship Church for helping me fulfill my purpose
- And finally, the National Speakers Association Central Florida Chapter for inspiring and educating me

PART I

OVERVIEW OF FRUSTRATION

F RUSTRATION WILL BE defined in two ways. You will be

- Made aware of the factors that impact the level of frustration that you experience
- Reassured that frustration is a natural part of life
- Given 7 assurances based on scripture to help you as you deal with day to day frustration

CHAPTER 1

Understanding Frustration

F RUSTRATION IS LIKE art. You know it when you feel it.
But to deal with it, you must use words. Frustration, like many words, has different meanings depending on who is using it and the context in which the person is using it.

The two most common definitions involve

- Unresolved problems—the lack of achieving a goal or something desired
- Unfulfilled needs—the deprivation of someone or something gratifying, desired, needed, and/or deserved

Whatever the cause, the emotional response of frustration must be dealt with in order to live a more calm, satisfying, and godly life.

The goals of this book are to help you understand that you don't have to live in a state of frustration and to help you remove it from your life using the wisdom of God's book, the Bible. The Bible is the place where God gives you the insights to comfort you and the solutions that will calm you.

A closer look at the causes and feelings associated with frustrations reveals that your level of frustration can vary. Many factors can influence its intensity, and you can determine that intensity by asking yourself the following five questions:

> The Bible is the place where God gives you the insights to comfort you and the solutions that will calm you.

1. How important is this to me?

People often say that their goals are important to them. However, they live their lives as if these things are not actually a major priority. For the most part, they don't experience a great amount of frustration when those aims do not become reality.

For example, think about New Year's resolutions. You may make them, but then experience very little stress or frustration when half the year is gone and you still have not lost the weight or started that exercise program you resolved to do. You may attend a conference, revival, or workshop and leave motivated to change. Yet a few months pass and you find you are still following the same routine but with very little regret.

On the other hand, if you have an interview for your dream job and you write down the wrong directions to get there, causing you to miss the interview, you feel a high degree of frustration.

2. How close was I to achieving the goal?

Frustration level can vary depending on how close a person is to reaching the goal. And it is usually higher the closer the person is to succeeding.

Have you ever failed for only a very small reason to get something you really wanted? You wonder, "What if . . . ?" Say, if you had just been ten minutes earlier? If you had gotten just two more answers correct on that test? If you had waited just a little while longer? If your credit score were just a little higher?

Faced with these kinds of possibilities, you would probably be experiencing a higher degree of frustration.

3. What is the cause of the frustration?

People can experience varying levels of frustration depending on the reason why they aren't achieving their goals. On one hand, they may tend to be more accepting and less frustrated when something beyond human control prevents them from reaching the goal. On the other hand, they may tend to be more frustrated when another person (or people) prevents them from achieving it.

For example, you spent the past hour pleading with your significant other to hurry so you can get to your child's eighth grade graduation. Then the phone rings and it's your significant other's best friend who does not understand that your significant other doesn't have time to talk. When you finally get to the graduation, you have missed your child's speech. Very frustrating situation, huh? How much different would your level of frustration be if the reason you missed your child's speech was due to a car accident that blocked traffic?

We tend to experience a greater degree of frustration with regards to people versus things or happenstance.

4. What was my level of frustration before this?

Everyone knows about the infamous scenario where someone has a frustrating day at work and then comes home and takes it out on the family. The fact of the matter is that the home situation is no more frustrating than usual. However, the frustrating day at work makes the bickering of the children more challenging and the barking of the dog more irritating.

In some cases, you may use the phrase "now that was the straw that broke the camel's back," which means that under different circumstances or as an isolated issue, the problem is not that bad. However, when you add it to a group of other issues, the frustration seems more than you can bear.

Isn't it amazing that something so small that would usually not bother you very much can cause an explosion because of other frustration you are already carrying around?

5. How many times and how long do I have to deal with this?

Knowing that a frustration will last just a certain length of time makes it a lot easier to handle. Most people are cognizant of the fact that, in life, things happen and people make mistakes. They can deal with having things go wrong every now and then, or when they know it is only for a short time.

Have you ever worked with someone during his or her last month until retirement? It is interesting to watch how things that would normally be a huge bother can be transformed into an "Oh well" response. Other workers are distressed and frustrated, but the soon-to-be retiree remains blasé and relaxed. This is because the retiree knows that the present situation will soon be over.

When relief from the situation is close, you can tolerate it a lot better.

Conclusion

When issues are

- of real importance
- just about the be realized
- within a person's control
- added on top of other frustrations
- frequent or long lasting,

people become less inclined to be patient or forgiving. Although this emotional reaction is normal, it can be very negative if it is prolonged. Unfortunately many folks describe their lives as constantly stressful, hectic, worrisome, and cumbersome. Circumstances in their lives are keeping them from being at peace.

God provides the way to be at peace—to feel calmness, contentment, serenity. It is important for each believer to know that being at peace does not mean that there is a lack of problems. On the contrary, being at peace is the attitude of well-being you as a believer can have as you face problems, difficulties, and disappointments because you know that Jesus promises you ultimate peace.

It is a fact that as long as you live, frustration will occur. It is also a fact that you don't have to, and you should not constantly, live in a state of frustration. You *can* learn to effectively deal with your personal frustration, and then to let it go.

CHAPTER 2

Reality: That's Life . . . What Did You Expect?

THE PAST FEW months have been extremely challenging for Sister Faith. "God, I don't know how much more I can take. Please help," she whispers on her way into the hospital where she has had to work extra hours due to short staffing.

She loves God, her family, their church, and the patients in the local hospital. However, trying to effectively be a mother, wife, only daughter to her recently widowed mother, Sunday school teacher, and part-time nurse is rather tough all at the same time.

Her two children are very active in the church as well as in sports and extracurricular activities. Her son Jonathan, an all-around athlete, excels at football and basketball. But Jonathan is having some trouble adjusting to a high school he was just re-zoned to, which most of his friends do not attend. Sister Faith has had conferences with all of Jonathan's teachers, his principal, and his guidance counselor, who thinks that Jonathan has an adjustment disorder, and recommends that Jonathan see a professional therapist.

Fortunately Sister Faith's daughter Janet, a senior, is still thriving. Her grades are superior, she has a great group of friends, and she is very active in the youth ministry and the church choir. Janet has been pleading for her own car for the past year. She frequently reminds her parents that she has not caused them any problems and that she always does what she is told, yet she can never drive anywhere on her own. Janet recently said to her mother, "Maybe I should start acting out like Jonathan; then you and dad will pay some attention to me."

Janet's statement caused Sister Faith to have a deep sense of guilt that she is not doing more for her daughter. Sister Faith would love nothing more than to grant her daughter's request. However, with the day-to-day financial demands of ministry along with saving for Janet to attend college, there is no room for a car payment in the family budget.

Sister Faith has noticed that she has become less patient and kind. She has dreaded going to work and even to church most days this month. Her blood pressure is elevated and she has been having headaches lately. She does not want to burden her husband because he is also stressed with working full time in addition to his responsibilities at the church. In fact, Sister Faith has been concerned about her husband's recent complaints of headaches and backaches. They promised each other they would see a doctor when things settled down.

Sister Faith has had a wake-up call. A young lady she teaches in Sunday school told her, "Ms. Faith we miss the old you. You have not been the same loving, fun person we enjoy being with in Sunday school."

This statement brought to mind advice her father gave her the day before he died. She distinctly remembers his gruff but weak voice saying, "Make sure you and mom never forget to sail." Sister Faith's dad loved the water and took his family sailing when Faith was young. He often told her and her mom, "You never know what the weather is going to be like nor which way the wind will blow, but if you know how to sail, you can use the wind to your advantage." It was advice for sailing and for life.

> Remember the old saying "Expect the unexpected." Recognizing this ahead of time is half the battle in handling frustrations successfully.

Looking back at the past few months, Sister Faith thinks about how she has allowed the storms and winds in her life to shake her up and cause her to spend each day worried and frustrated rather than sailing through the storms in her life. Sister Faith says to herself, "Wow, just how many days do I spend being frustrated? If the girls in my Sunday school class have noticed it, I am sure others at home, church, and work have noticed it as well." She whispers another quick prayer. "God, forgive me for not giving my troubles and frustrations to you and for not walking and living in your peace and joy."

How many times do you find yourself like Sister Faith being so caught up in the cares of life that you spend days, weeks, and months frustrated because you are affected by unforeseen and challenging circumstances? Remember the old saying "Expect the unexpected." It

DR. ADRIAN MANLEY

will help you to adjust to "expecting" to have changing and challenging circumstances that you have to deal with—in other words, real life. Recognizing this ahead of time is half the battle in handling them successfully.

Expectation

Has anyone ever asked you, "What did you expect?" You can be thrown off kilter and experience frustrations because something is totally different from what you expected. I distinctly remember learning this lesson in kindergarten. The teacher had a bag of chocolate and told us we could have as much as we wanted but we had to eat it all. Of course, like many other of my classmates, I dug in expecting to taste creamy sweet chocolate. To our surprise we had a mouth full of creamy *unsweetened* chocolate.

Thirty years later I still remember what that bitter surprise taught me: things don't always turn out the way I expect them to. I'm sure you have had a few surprises when, even though you had realistic expectations, things did not happen as expected. Having realistic expectations is a good thing; however, we need to clearly understand that in life we don't always get everything we anticipate, and we should be prepared to effectively deal with this fact.

On the other hand, some people are constantly frustrated because their expectations are idealistic and unrealistic. I am privileged to work as a counselor at a state college. I get to see many young adults take their first venture into adulthood. It is interesting to observe youngsters who are fresh out of high school experience life as an adult. I enjoy helping create moments when students can broaden their ideas, thoughts, notions, and expectations about life through interacting with people whose lives and lifestyles are vastly different from their own.

It can be very easy for adolescents to limit their thinking based on their fortunate and sometimes sheltered lives growing up. When some of my students face the reality of adult responsibility, consequences, and choices, it is a big and sometimes rude awakening. The truth is that everyone has expectations about family, money, ministry, and life in general. Let's explore this in further detail.

Life's situations, circumstances, issues, and problems

People have certain beliefs, ideas, and philosophies about life. If you examine your ideologies, you will likely find that your expectations for life are rooted in them. However, some life experiences will not fit with your beliefs and expectations. As you try to make sense of what is going on, you realize that in order for things to work well, you may have to modify your thinking.

As I have assisted couples and individuals in counseling, I have made a list of some problematic expectations and mistaken beliefs that many people start out with.

- All parents love their children and do what is best for them.
- If I try harder, my abusive significant other will stop abusing me.
- When people make marriage vows, they will do their best to keep them.
- If I am a really good spouse, I will have a really good relationship.
- If I am a good person, everything will go well for me.
- If I don't bother people, people won't bother me.
- What you don't do today you can do tomorrow.
- Everyone is treated fairly.
- My age, race, socioeconomic status, and past will stop me from achieving major goals.
- Bad things happen only to bad people.

Perhaps one or two statements on the list above spoke directly to one or two of your life situations or a time when you had a great awakening. Life is full of wonderful experiences that bring us, joy, happiness, and success. Writers throughout history have referred to these kinds of experiences as mountaintop experiences, or bright and sunshiny days. Thank God for these moments and never forget them. Make sure to celebrate and enjoy the wonderful moments of life to the fullest. However, realize that not all of life's moments are going to be wonderful.

The ten beliefs above are ideals. But this is not an ideal world. In this world crime, hate, social injustice, and strife are part of our daily living, as are sorrow, sadness, and disappointment. As long as you live, you will encounter challenges, conflict, problems, and frustration. God does not take these situations away, but He shows you how to deal with them. The key is to expect them, and be prepared to deal with them.

DR. ADRIAN MANLEY

Life, like competitive sports, requires preparedness. In fact, even the apostle Paul used the metaphor of winning a race. As you read this chapter, think about competitive sports in general. In fact, think about your personal favorite sport.

> As long as you live, you will encounter challenges, conflict, problems, and frustration. God shows you how to deal with them. The key is to expect them, and be prepared to deal with them.

Wise athletes know that if they are going to have any chance in competitive sports, they must commit sufficient time to conditioning and training. Athletes work very hard because they know that their opponents are also working very hard to triumph over them. They realize that success will not be easy.

My brothers and sisters, in life you have an opponent, an adversary—the devil. Paul instructed the church in Ephesus to *be strong in the Lord and in his mighty power. Put on the full armor of God so that you can take your stand against the devil's schemes.* Ephesians 6:10-11. Several other scriptures inform the believer that there will be problems, suffering, disappointment, and even persecution. Peter writes, *Dear friends, do not be surprised at the painful trial you are suffering, as though something strange were happening to you.* 1 Peter 4:12.

Yet, as humans we many times tend to have the natural response of being alarmed and disoriented when we face trouble. Sometimes we even say, "I can't believe this is happening to me" or "I never thought this would happen to me." You must condition your mind and attitude to realize that discouragement, obstacles, and even tragedies will happen in your life. You must be equipped with the armor of God along with prayer and fasting. With these necessary components the believer is guaranteed to endure and triumph over anything that comes along.

Always remember who you are and who you have inside you. John writes that believers have the greater one living inside of them. *The one who is in you is greater than the one who is in the world* (the antichrist). 1John 4:4. Without a doubt there is not anyone or anything greater than our God.

In the Bible God gives you 7 assurances to help you face life's harsh realities.

God's 7 Assurances No Matter What You Go Through

1. **Nothing will happen in your life that you can't bear.** 1 Corinthians 10:13 declares *And God is faithful; he will not let you to be tempted beyond what you can bear. But when you are tempted, he will also provide a way out so that you can stand up under it.* It is encouraging and reassuring to know that God will faithfully make a way for you to go through anything that comes your way.

2. **Jesus understands and is ready to help you.** Hebrews 4:15-16 affirms this. *For we do not have a high priest who is unable to sympathize with our weaknesses, but we have one who has been tempted in every way, just as we are—yet was without sin. Let us then approach the throne of grace with confidence, so that we may receive mercy and find grace to help us in our time of need.*

   Have you ever tried getting help from someone who hindered your progress more than he or she actually helped you? For example, you may have had a repair or a small problem and called a friend or family member who couldn't get the job done. In those times you could say that it was time to "call a professional." Some matters are just too complex for Uncle Joe to fix, and you need someone who is trained, capable, and qualified to handle them. Jesus, our great high priest, is the Professional Helper you can call to assist you in any problematic situation in your life.

3. **Nothing will happen unless God allows it.** In Psalm 31:15a David writes, *My times are in your hands.* God is in control of what happens to everyone. Up times, down times, happy times, and sad times are all predicated upon what God will and won't allow to transpire in life. Everything that happens passes through the "God filter." Yes, everything that comes along has to go through God first.

   Therefore HE is not surprised or caught off guard by the things you struggle with at any time in your life. If he allows it to happen, he has a reason, and according Romans 8:28, *And we know that in all things God works for the good of those who love him, who have been called according to his purpose.* It will work out for your good, even though only God may know how at the moment. Nothing catches God by surprise. He had a plan to work things out before there was even a problem.

4. **You are not in it alone; God is right there with you.** You have many promises that God is with you. In Matthew 28:20b Jesus says, *And surely I am with you always, to the very end of the age.* This confirms Hebrews 13:5—*God has said, Never will I leave you; never will I forsake you.*

   I am having the time of my life with my three-year-old and one-year-old sons. One of my own personal lessons learned from parenting is that my children have an extra sense of security when Daddy is present. Anytime they are frightened, they make it to daddy's arms, and just as I scoop them up, they turn around to look at and face what frightened them. As Christians you should find encouragement in knowing that your Father is with you and for you. As long as HE is with you, you have what it takes and who it takes to meet any challenge. For example, when you lose loved ones you counted on to help you, and you feel a void when they are no longer present, you can rest assured and be less frustrated because God is with you.

5. **You can still have peace and joy.** Psalm 119:143 states *Trouble and distress have come upon me, but your commands give me delight.* In essence the writer says that during stressful and high pressured times, we can find joy in the word of God. Isaiah 26:3 declares, *You will keep in perfect peace whose minds are steadfast, because they trust in you.*

   Paul wrote in Philippians 4:7, *And the peace of God, which transcends all understanding, will guard your hearts and your minds in Christ Jesus.* God has the ability to give you peace in the midst of the storms in your life. James 1:2 encourages believers to *Consider it pure joy, my brothers and sisters, whenever you face trials of many kinds.* We don't rejoice about our problems; we rejoice that we have a God who is the ultimate problem solver. We can be at peace knowing that God is taking care of it all. It's just a matter of going through the process.

   > We don't rejoice about our problems; we rejoice that we have a God who is the ultimate problem solver.

6. **God still loves us.** In Romans 8:38-39 the Apostle Paul writes, *For I am convinced that neither death nor life, neither angels nor*

demons, neither the present nor the future, nor any powers, neither height nor depth, nor anything else in all creation, will be able to separate us from the love of God that is in Christ Jesus our Lord. When I first read, that scripture, I thought that Paul was saying nothing could stop him from loving God. I still remember the difference it made when I realized the apostle was saying that nothing could ever stop God (in Christ Jesus) from loving us.

It led me back to the childhood scripture of John 3:16 declaring, *For God so loved the world that he gave his one and only Son, that whoever believes in him shall not perish but have eternal life.* What blessing it is to know that God has always loved us, God loves us now, and God will always love us.

7. **We have something great to look forward to in the future.** Psalm 30:5 informs us that *Weeping may stay for the night, but rejoicing comes in the morning.* No matter how long or dark the night, morning is coming.

Paul shares with the Roman believers in Romans 8:18 that *I consider that our present sufferings are not worth comparing with the glory that will be revealed in us.* What a comforting scripture. You can have great joy in knowing your past and present pain is not worth comparing to God's personal promise of an amazing future. Things will get better!

Conclusion

Let's face it, Frustration happens. You are constantly faced with situations, circumstances, issues, and problems that hinder or stop you from achieving a goal or something desired. It is only human to experience feeling deprived of someone or something that was gratifying, desired, needed, and/or deserved at various times in life. But re-examine your expectations and the role they play in your frustration. Finally, you have 7 assurances from God to comfort you as you deal with daily frustrations.

Understanding that day-to-day experiences and expectations are at the root of frustration is preparation for the next chapters which look at specific areas in life where frustration occurs.

PART II

TYPES OF FRUSTRATION

F RUSTRATION OCCURS IN all areas of life. You will be

- Made aware of where it occurs
- Shown examples of how it occurs
- Given strategies for dealing with it

CHAPTER 3

Family Frustration

FAMILY MEMBERS CAN be a tremendous source of stress and frustration in life. As hard as it can be to admit, these people whom you love so dearly can frustrate you, maybe more than anyone else. Families are intricate, complex, and difficult systems. No matter how things appear on the outside, families have problems, dysfunctional aspects, drama, secrets, and issues. It would be marvelous if the following assertions were true:

- My children are going to completely obey me and never do anything that I think is dangerous or bad.
- My spouse is going fully understand my needs, desires, and feelings.
- My siblings are going be perfect people and give me full support when I need it.
- My parents are going to live forever and be healthy all the days of their lives.
- My in-laws will be as loving, compromising, patient, and understanding as my spouse.

Maybe these statements sound unrealistic now that you are reading them in this book. Yet many people are frustrated because things are not what they want or expect them to be in their own family. There's something about the people you love the most that gives them a greater likelihood to cause the most frustration in your life. Let's examine some specific family dynamics.

PARENT-CHILD FRUSTRATION

- My children listen to their friends instead of their parents.
- My children may be drinking, smoking, or doing drugs.
- My children may not remain celibate until marriage.
- My children have friends that I disapprove of.
- My children don't appreciate my efforts to keep them on the right track.

Children can be a cause of frustration in the lives of parents. Yes, those cute, smart individuals whom you love so much can be great sources of frustration. As parents you have high hopes, expectations, and dreams for your children. You want them to go further in life than you have gone. You want them to make the right decisions and be successful. You want them to live on their own without having to depend on anyone. You want them to hang around the right crowd, get a good education, and choose the right significant other. In some cases you may have your children's lives planned out. Then reality happens.

Yes, the reality is that your children are going to mess up and make some bad decisions, just as you may have done in the past. Sometimes parents tend to lose touch with the issues and challenges they faced in their own childhood. Remember that one of the greatest teachers is experience. This old saying is still true: You learn good judgment from your bad judgment.

People learn either from the mistakes of others or from their own sometimes painful mistakes. Likewise, children will have to learn some lessons the hard way. And some people learn more quickly than others.

> The reality is that your children are going to mess up and make some bad decisions, just as you may have done in the past.

Another issue is that parents have the tendency to want to fix things for their children. However, there is only so much parents can do and only so far they can, or should, go for their children.

Wisdom ~ Five Tips for Parents Dealing with Frustration

1. **Don't expect children, especially teens, to behave as adults.**
   Although it is going to seem they don't want you around or need

you around, they need you. Yes, it is going to feel like they care more about what their friends say than what you say. But lovingly and firmly tell them what they need to know.

2. **Know when to stop talking to them and start talking to God about them.** Aka: Stop fussing and start praying (especially with adult children). Adult children are still adults, even though they are their parents' children. It is an interesting situation for both sides of this relationship. As their children grow older, parents must adjust their parenting styles. God can see the children when no one else can. God can reach them when no one else can. God can protect them when no one else can. So, pray, pray, pray, and let God do what He does best.

3. **Remember Jesus! He loves us continuously even with all our flaws. So too we should love our children continuously and make sure they know it, even when we don't approve of their lifestyles or decisions.** Jesus is the best example. He loves you through your faults, failures, and hang-ups. If Jesus can love you in spite of your imperfections, you can love your children. Tell them you love them often.

> Jesus loves us continuously even with all our flaws. So too we should love our children continuously and make sure they know it.

4. **Be the kind of person and the kind of parent you want your children to be.** They are looking at you. They are looking at the relationships in your home. They are looking at how you handle things. It amazing how much your environment and the people in your environment, especially parents, affect children of any age.

5. **No enabling; be careful about stressing yourself out trying to protect them from the very thing that may be their wake-up call.** You just may be the one who helps keep an unhealthy cycle going. For parents, one of the hardest things is not jumping in and fixing the situation or covering up their children's mess-ups. Too much of this does not help you or your children.

CHILD-PARENT FRUSTRATION

- Dad will always be strong an independent.
- I will always be able to go get advice from mom.

- I will be able to care for my parents as they age.
- My parents will be able to financially support themselves.
- My parents will be well cared for with a united effort from all of their children.

More than ever adult children are becoming responsible for taking care of their parents. This is a tremendous source of frustration. Seeing their parents' health decline to the point they are unable to take care of themselves takes a toll on any loving child.

Many times matters are complicated even more when there is a loss of one parent. In the case when one parent dies, it is often necessary for the children to step in to help. Some struggle with whether to move to be closer to parents or whether to move parents in with them. Financial matters, health issues, loneliness, along with normal adjustment and transition issues can cause daily frustration.

Still, matters are further complicated when there are multiple children. Families become frustrated that all children don't pull their fair share of responsibility for parental care. In many cases it is one child who takes on the responsibility for caring for the parent. Some adult children don't have the means necessary to care for their parents. Some adult children feel as though their sibling does not take proper care of their parent. Some even feel like one child may take too much from their parent. Other delicate issues can include having the parent be responsible for babysitting grandchildren or even vice versa. Many dynamics can come in to play that are very frustrating for adult children with a parent or parents who have health problems.

Wisdom ~ Five Tips for Adult Children Dealing with Frustration

1. **Be thankful** that you can return the favor for all your parents did for you and show them your love and support.
2. **Be prayerful**—when you are feeling overwhelmed, unload on God.
3. **Be honest** about how much you can handle and how you feel.
4. **Be collaborative**—ask for help and involve in the process others who love your parents.
5. **Be mindful**—take care of yourself, take breaks, take time to renew and replenish *you.*

SPOUSE FRUSTRATION

- I shouldn't have to tell you that.
- You should have known I did not want that.
- You should see that I need some TLC (Tender Loving Care).
- You should understand.
- If you would(n't) do that, then I would(n't) be doing this.

I am always amazed that couples expect their spouses to know, understand, and do things without any communication. It was a lesson I learned early when dating my wife.

She and I were returning from a five-hour trip. I admit that I am the guy who doesn't like to stop on a road trip. About halfway into the trip my then girlfriend mentioned in the course of casual conversation (so I thought) that her throat was getting dry. I kept talking about the topic we were discussing before she mentioned her throat, and of course I kept driving. Two hours later she said in a very sarcastic tone, "I guess I can't get anything to drink." I said, "Sure you can. Why didn't you say you wanted me to stop and get something to drink?" She reminded me about her earlier statement. Confused, I asked when that was. She had hurt feelings in her voice: "two hours ago I told you my throat was dry. You should have at least offered to stop then."

Why didn't she just ask? In her opinion, her communication was clear that she wanted to stop and get something to drink. I had no clue she wanted to stop. You can probably recall a similar situation where someone communicated what he or she thought was a clear message and someone else totally missed it. Yes, with time we should learn more about our spouses. We should become knowledgeable about their likes, dislikes, values, attitudes, moods, and pet peeves, and we should deal with them in a positive way.

In addition, it is important to remember that we and others have different needs at different times.

For example, John always seems to find pleasure in going to a favorite restaurant. So one day his wife Jane decides to surprise him. She arranges for a babysitter, leaves work early, and is ready to take John out on Friday evening. However, John's week at work has been so hectic that he just wants to stay home and crash. Jane is offended, disappointed, and frustrated. She has made all these plans only to find him home on the couch for the night.

To further complicate matters, Jane doesn't communicate her feelings when she finds John settled in on the couch. After canceling the babysitter, she tells John to watch the kids and goes upstairs to take a nap.

What should she have done differently? A simple matter of communication could have prevented this frustration from happening. Jane could have sent John an e-mail or a text, or called him to say not to make plans because she had a special surprise for him.

It is vital that spouses stay connected to what is going on in each others' lives, and how these things are impacting them. Because spouses are so interconnected, what greatly affects one will ultimately affect the other. When one spouse is stressed, frustrated, angry, resentful, or hurt, it cannot help but affect the other spouse and the relationship they share.

Always make the time and effort to honestly and openly communicate about your thoughts and feelings with your spouse. If you do not communicate in this manner, you will likely experience a great degree of frustration and a steady drifting apart. Never be too busy to seek, know, and understand what is important to your spouse. Strive to be keenly aware of what is happening on your spouse's job, with his or her family, and with mental and physical health. *Pay attention to your spouse now, or pay for it later!*

It is also important to work with your spouse as the individual that person is and not who you want that person to be. One of the worst mistakes you can make is to compare your spouse or marriage to another person or marriage. For some reason, even as adults, people get deceived by what they see on television. Many couples still get their cues about the various components of marriage from their favorite movie or television couple, especially in the areas of intimacy and romance. One of the smartest things a couple can do is see each other and the relationship for what they really are and strive to make it better.

Wisdom ~ Five Tips for Spouses Dealing with Frustration

1. **Make sure you know what your spouse expects from you and your spouse knows what you expect from him or her.** You will save yourself from frustration and aggravation when you communicate your needs, desires, wants, and feelings rather than expecting your spouse to just know these things.

2. **Be willing to change your expectations.** Sometimes the best thing or best person to change is you. Yes, with some things you learn to accept and stop allowing them to frustrate you.

3. **Be able to identify, focus on, and work on the actions that cause frustration.** Are you frustrated because your spouse is lazy or because the household chores are not getting done? You could act out and call your spouse lazy, or you could find ways of getting the chores done. When possible, don't attribute your frustration to your spouse, but to an action or situation. You will have more success changing actions and situations than by trying to change your spouse.

4. **Expect your spouse to be your spouse, not someone else.** Don't sabotage your relationship by comparing your spouse with others. Don't be frustrated by
   > Expect your spouse to be your spouse, not someone else.

   unrealistic expectations. Learn how to deal with your spouse for who he or she is and with his or her own personality.

5. **The two of you take a vacation, staycation, or daycation, and have fun with each other.** You know that when two people have fun together, frustrations decrease. It doesn't have to be expensive. Before you say you can't afford to do it, ask yourself a more important question: can you afford not to do it?

SIBLING FRUSTRATION

- My sister needs to get her act together.
- My brother is always borrowing money.
- I never know what my sister will do next.
- My brother should move out.
- Our parents need more help from my sister.

Sibling frustration can be very cumbersome. It is easy for adults reflecting on their childhood to remember certain inequalities among their siblings. Whether it was the inequality of privileges, gifts, or discipline, siblings sometimes believe that parents loved or liked a certain sibling more than others. Past sibling rivalry is an issue in many families. What happens as those siblings grow into adulthood? Can a sibling be a source frustration?

Frustration, strife, jealousy, and even hatred can exist among siblings. One source of frustration between siblings is how differently their parents treat them, even as adults. Some siblings are very independent and successful. Their parents don't feel the need to give them much. On the other hand, some siblings seem to be constantly needy. Their parents give them money, gifts, and even a place to stay for lengthy periods of time. The independent adult children may feel that their parents are letting themselves be taken advantage of by other adult children. In some cases siblings accuse other siblings of using their parents and being a source of stress to the parents.

Another major source of frustration involves how differently siblings treat their parents. Some siblings are frustrated about how often their siblings do or don't call, visit, or care for their parents. As parents age and experience health issues, their children are often called on to assist. These situations usually end up with one sibling doing much more to care for parents and one or more others doing much less. Frustration tends to rise as siblings come together to look at who has the money, who has the time, who lives closer—and who is doing most of the work.

Finally, some siblings still struggle with sibling rivalry that has nothing to do with their parents. They constantly look at what another sibling or other siblings have and how it compares to them. Or they constantly brag about what they do, what they have, and how much they have done, even using family gatherings as a time to make themselves appear better or better off than other siblings.

Wisdom ~ Five Tips for Dealing with Sibling Frustration

1. **Show love to your siblings** and be there for them as much as you can.
2. **Remember—parents know their children.** Sometimes they give a certain child more because they know that specific child needs more. If you are not receiving things from your parents, take it as a compliment that you can do well without their assistance.
3. **Do as much as you can** for your parents to the best of your ability. Don't expect other siblings to do what you do.
4. **Remember the only person you can control is you.** Don't try to control siblings.

> Pray for your siblings. When talking to them won't work, talk to God about them.

DR. ADRIAN MANLEY

5. **Pray for your siblings.** When talking to them won't work, talk to God about them.

IN-LAW FRUSTRATION

- I don't want to spend holidays with them.
- I don't like the way they talk to you.
- They make me feel like a stranger.
- They know too much of our business.
- I don't like them, and I don't trust them.

Life is frustrating enough without in-laws who fit the stereotype. Has anyone ever told you that when you marry someone you marry the family as well? That statement may not be completely true; however, it is true that the family you were raised in plays a big role in your life both before and after you are married. Although that role may change after marriage, it is nonetheless a big one. Caring relatives don't want to feel like they are losing a loved one when marriage occurs. It can be very difficult for both the married couple and their family groups to negotiate and renegotiate roles and boundaries after a marriage.

Frustration often occurs when relatives do not get the time, attention, and consideration they feel they should be given. Another common frustration crops up when family members don't like the way someone else is being treated. Finally, another source of frustration arises when one spouse feels like he or she is has to choose between his or her spouse and other family.

Wisdom ~ Five Tips for Dealing with Frustration with In-laws

1. **Define and set clear boundaries with your spouse.** Make sure you discuss how you want to be treated and how far you two will let things go.

2. **Make time to spend with family,** especially when grandchildren are involved.

> Remember that just because you are in love with a person, that does not mean your family is in love with that person.

3. **Remember that just because you are in love with a person, that does not mean your family is in love with that person.** *Don't give family members reasons to dislike your spouse.* Be careful what you share with them because they don't forgive as readily as you do.
4. **When there are problems, each spouse should deal with his or her own family members.**
5. **Give more respect than you get, though the balance should not be too far off.** No matter which side you are on, be at least as respectful as your spouse.

Conclusion

Family issues, challenges, and problems are prevalent in every family. Remember that your family is not the only one with issues. Whether it is finances, drugs, death, divorce, deceit, incarceration, infidelity, or simple arguments, all families experience frustration. Remembering and utilizing the tips and bits of wisdom in this chapter will help you release family frustration. Do what you can to help your family. And while you are doing it, love and pray for your family.

CHAPTER 4

Workplace Frustration

- I have a headache every time I go to work.
- These people should just do their jobs.
- This guy is a micro manager.
- It seems everybody is being promoted but me.
- I wish I could just go to work, do my job, and go home.

CONSIDER THIS SCENARIO of four friends after work. Johnny, Larry, Bob, and Bill decide to meet after work to watch the game at the local sports bar and grill. They have a while before the game starts, so Johnny asks the others how things are going at their jobs.

Larry starts by talking about problems with his employees at work. He states that he is not a micromanager, but his employees are a constant source of stress in his life. Larry is the new kid on the block; everyone else has been there at least three years and is accustomed to a certain work ethic and style. He never has enough employee coverage because people are always taking off or calling in sick. Furthermore, Larry often comes in to work early and leaves late so that he can have time to complete the work of others. Larry is constantly frustrated trying to have a more productive and professional workplace.

Bob chimes in about his supervisor who is a restrictive micromanager obsessed with his job. Bob shares that a year ago, before this new manager came, he really liked his job. Now he is completely frustrated every day, knowing this person is constantly looking over his shoulder.

Finally Bill has his say. Bill expresses frustration and resentment that he has been at the same level doing the same thing for the past five years. Bill states that he joined this company because there was room and opportunity for growth. Yet he has not moved up. Bill adds that he is not in with the in crowd and therefore gets overlooked for promotions.

"Wow," Johnny replies, "you guys really sound miserable. Do you really experience this much frustration in your jobs each day?" Larry, Bob, and Bill respond together with a resounding "YES!" Johnny smiles at his friends. "That means you each have work to do. First, start by asking yourselves two questions: (1) What am I doing or not doing to contribute to my workplace frustration? and (2) What is the best thing for me to do in order to decrease my workplace frustration?"

Frustration with Employees—Larry

Supervising and management can bring its share of rewards and frustrations. Larry has experienced his share of them in the past year. Most managers and supervisors have their specific tasks which require time and attention. In addition, they have people working under them who have their own tasks and personal issues. All of these factors can be considered the responsibility of the manager or supervisor.

In relation to Johnny's first question, Larry realizes that he could make his communication with the people working for him more creative, clear, and concise. He could employ productive and firm ways of explaining expectations, the rewards for meeting them, and the consequences for not meeting them. Rather than internalizing and doing things himself, he should be communicating with his team.

In relation to Johnny's second question about decreasing the frustration, Larry could employ the attitude and mindset of a coach. This approach involves several premises. First, a coach is not concerned with making people do what he or she wants them to do, but rather getting the team to work together for a win. In addition, the coach is motivational and inspirational, even when being strict for the good of the team. Finally, many leaders are hired for what they can bring to the organization or department, and to act as an agent of change in the department. Larry could seek innovative ways of decreasing the amount of time taken off and increasing work production.

DR. ADRIAN MANLEY

Frustration with the Manager—Bob

Anyone who works a significant amount of time will deal with a manager whose style and personality are frustrating. For an employee this can make life at work challenging to say the least. First, in considering what he is doing or not doing to contribute to his workplace frustration with his manager, Bob could examine himself to make sure that he is performing at a high enough level that his supervisor will truly have no need of constantly looking over his shoulder.

Second, in thinking about how to decrease job frustration that stems from his manager, Bob, like Larry, recognizes that clear and concise communication is key. As an employee, he realizes that it would be good to know how well he is performing his job. Most micromanagers are eager to talk to employees about how they can improve their work performance. So Bob could schedule a time to meet with his supervisor about his work performance. This would give Bob a chance to see and hear what his supervisor really thinks about his work.

Frustration with Stagnation—Bill

Stagnation is one of the most frustrating things in the world for someone who is ready to move forward. Feeling stuck in a certain position, pay grade, or department causes a great degree of frustration among employees. In contemplating Johnny's first question about how he might be contributing to his own frustration, Bill could identify and examine the cause of stagnation. He could make a list of the qualifications, character traits, and skills required for advancement. Then he could make a corresponding list of the ways he meets those criteria, just to be sure that he isn't standing in the way of his own progress.

Bill's effort to decrease his frustration, as a follow-up to Johnny's second question, could be to express his desire for advancement directly to his supervisor. Bill could effectively emphasize his desire for growth and the opportunity to be promoted. He could ask what specifics would be required for him to move to the next level. Finally, Bill may need to move on and look elsewhere for employment. It is true that in some organizations, your way up is going to be by getting out of that organization.

Johnny—The Wise Friend

You may find yourself playing the role of Johnny with some of your friends and colleagues. In such cases, take note of Johnny's technique. First Johnny listens to each friend share his frustration. Never underestimate the power of letting people vent to a great listener. Next Johnny encourages self-reflection and action. Sometimes we can forget to take a good look within when we are faced with frustrating situations. Finally, Johnny encourages friends to determine the best course of action and follow through with it.

A rough time in the economy causes many workers to lose their jobs. There are thousands of people who need and want a job. So the

> Sometimes we can forget to take a good look within when we are faced with frustrating situations.

very first way to address job frustration is to be thankful that you are employed. Imagine what it would be like to go to work tomorrow and find out you no longer have a job. Unfortunately, some lose their homes, cars, and others their personal possessions for want of a job—any job. It's good to be grateful for what you have.

That being said, frustration is real and must be dealt with. What is your job frustration? Is it a case of too much? Too much work, too much stress, too much favoritism. Or is it a case of too little? Too little pay, too little appreciation, too little time off. Whatever the case, there is a way to deal with the frustration on your job.

Wisdom ~ Five Tips for Dealing with Frustration on Your Job

1. **Every day you work, start with prayer.** In your prayer, thank God for allowing you to have a job. Thank God for the ability to work. Deuteronomy 8:18a states, *But remember the LORD your God, for it is he that gives you the ability to produce wealth.* Spend time praying for the people at your job. Spend even more time praying for yourself. Pray for your attitude. Ask God to help you do your very best.

2. **Do the best job you can.** Some job frustration comes from what we do or don't do right on the job. If you are doing your best, then you will make fewer mistakes, have high quality production, be timely and efficient, and treat others with decency,

tact, and respect. Doing these things will diminish a great deal of job frustration. Don't expect favors; work hard to earn your promotion, raise, etc.

3. **Make a special effort to communicate effectively on your job.** When something needs to be addressed, address it at the right time in the right way to the right person. Be careful not to offend, and if you do, quickly apologize and make changes to your behavior. In many cases, great communication skills can decrease frustration.

4. **Be a part of the solution.** There will be problems at all jobs. Expect them and prepare yourself to be a part of the solution and not a part of the problem. Be helpful and supportive of others: you spend a lot of time on the job with your coworkers. Do your part to make your workplace a good environment. The key to decreasing your workplace frustration could simply be a matter of your stepping up to be a part of the solution.

5. **Know when it is time to move on.** Don't act hastily in anger or frustration, and never allow people to run you away. Carefully and thoughtfully weigh out your options, make your decision, and lay out a plan. In some cases, it is time to look for employment elsewhere. However, make sure that you have learned all you need to know and have performed at a top quality level where you are before you make your next move. In addition, have a solid plan in place. In essence, you should outgrow your current position rather just leaving it.

Conclusion

We spend so much of our time in the workplace. It is worth our time and effort to minimize workplace frustration. There will always be issues, changes, and challenges in the workplace. Using the godly wisdom in this chapter will help you decrease and effectively deal with your workplace frustration.

CHAPTER 5

Church Frustration

- Ministry should not be this difficult.
- Parishioners will pay attention to the messages in the sermons and apply them to their lives.
- We should all just get along.
- Everybody will pull together and contribute his or her fair share.
- The pastor should not make mistakes.

CONSIDER THIS SCENARIO. It is after one of those notorious business meetings. You know—the ones where tough conversations that should have occurred a year ago finally happen. It is easy to see and hear the frustrations of people at all levels.

The pastor is taken aback at all the issues people are addressing that he did not know about. He tried to organize a committee to address some of those issues, but no one stepped forward to help, so he dropped the issues. The pastor is also discouraged to hear some issues are still unsettled after he has taught a twelve-week series focusing on them. The pastor thinks to himself, "I just spent time teaching and preaching about Godly communication, being in unity, and staying your lane. Where were these people for the past twelve weeks? How could this be?" Is he that out of touch with his congregation? Is he not being effective in his teaching and preaching?

The head of the financial committee leaves the meeting upset. Giving and tithing are lower than they have been in the past five years, but the people are complaining that they want the church to do more. He murmurs to himself, "They give less and want more. Don't they understand that the church is able to do what we need based on what we are given?"

The assistant pastor leaves the meeting after trying desperately to steer the meeting toward looking for a solution versus having a gripe session. He thinks to himself, "The people who complain the most are the ones who do the least. They never step up and volunteer to make things better. Every time I am asked to get committees to help, people never fully participate. I am only one person."

A group of three members meets over coffee after the meeting. The topic of their discussion is the leadership of the church. One person says, "If they would actually ask me for help, I would be happy to contribute my expertise. But they have the same few people doing everything so I just stopped trying." Another person chimes saying, "Yeah, the pastor has his special people that he likes to do everything. I bet he doesn't know all the expertise and skill we have sitting at this table. They need help but they are too dumb to know it." Finally the third person agrees, stating, "I could really bring this church up to par. God gives me all kinds of revelations, and I know just what we need. But do they ask me? No."

As we examine the monologues and the dialogue regarding the business meeting, let's look at varying types of frustration people experience in the church.

Frustration with Leadership

Church leadership is complex for various reasons. Some lead because they feel they are called and anointed to lead. Some lead because they are asked to lead. Others lead because they feel forced to lead. Some leaders have extensive training to lead. Other leaders have almost no training to lead. In many churches, leaders are afforded a salary so that they have time, energy, and resources to give to the church. However, other churches are not set up to compensate leaders to have the work of the church be their full-time job. So these people in essence volunteer their time and talent to assist when and how they can. How much can one pastor with a full-time job and family of four do? How much does his church expect him to be able to do?

Pastors are still people. Some congregants forget that. This statement is in no way intended to give church leaders a permit for immoral, unethical, sinful, and ungodly lifestyles. Pastors should, in fact, maintain higher moral standards than the average person. They should live a lifestyle that reflects Jesus Christ. The statement that pastors are still people is meant to address limitations in ability, energy, knowledge, and skill, and definitely not in behavior. It also acknowledges that people make mistakes. People who expect pastors, or anyone, to be perfect will experience disappointment and frustration. Pastors need prayer and supportive, loving people working with them.

Wisdom ~ Five Tips for Dealing with Frustration with Leadership

1. **Pray, Pray, Pray for your church leadership.** Pastors are human, and church leadership is not as easy as it seems. Leaders need the Holy Spirit to lead them. Pastors are not God; they are people called by God. Make prayer your first response.
2. **Make sure you can and do respect your church leadership.** If you have leadership that you cannot respect, you need to pray to determine if you are in the right congregation.
3. **Communicate with your leadership.** Don't just write or state complaints. Talk about concerns, and also about things that are going well.
4. **Volunteer.** Many leaders don't have the time to survey the congregation to see whom to place over a project. They pick those who have demonstrated interest and ability to get the job done. Make church leadership aware of your spiritual gifts and natural talents and skills and offer to use them in the service of the Lord.
5. **Be a good example to others** by making sure you are not a part of the problem and you don't add to the problem.

Be a good example to others.

Frustration with Followers

Church leadership is more difficult than workplace leadership in many ways. Within the workplace, employees get a salary, raises, bonuses, and benefits. In the church, many followers get a thank you and God bless you.

It is true that a great number of church members get the benefits of altruism and the satisfaction that they are working with Christ to build his kingdom. Is this enough to keep people committed and dedicated to the work of a particular church congregation? For many it is enough to keep them motivated to the cause of Christ, but it is not enough to keep them motivated to deal with the issues of church work. Therefore leaders get frustrated at the lack of commitment and motivation of church members.

Leaders experience a great degree of frustration when their followers quit, leave, and fail to honor their commitments. It can happen for a variety of reasons. Some church members overcommit because they are caught up in the moment. It's like buyers' remorse when they get something they can't afford. While it is easy to take something back to the store, it is more difficult to go back and say, "I can't do what I said I would do." Therefore some just slowly quit showing up.

Many people stop honoring their commitments due to the unexpected challenges, hurt, and negativity they receive from others. For some reason people think that working in the church should be the easiest thing in the world. It is almost heart-breaking when people find out the hard way that church work is hard work and that some people are difficult to deal with even though they go to church. When church members stop fulfilling their duties, the leaders are left once again to try to figure out how to carry on the work.

Finally, some members have idiosyncrasies that make working with them difficult. Some never volunteer; they want you to seek them out. Others are pessimists and full of negativity. Some are just lack proper knowledge and training. They don't know how to communicate and work as a team. Some think they know it all—even more than the leader. Others think that there is only one way to do things—theirs. These are all issues that leaders must be prepared to deal with concerning church members. Leaders should expect these issues and prepare themselves to effectively deal with them and the members they lead.

Wisdom ~ Five Tips for Dealing with Frustration with Followers

1. **Strive to make your followers into leaders.** Invest in training and teaching followers what they need to know to be good followers and leaders. People cannot do what they don't know to do.

> Strive to make your followers into leaders.

2. **Seek training on dealing with difficult people.** Sometimes as a leader you need to adjust your technique rather than expecting your followers to adjust to you.
3. **Love people and let them know you care about them.** If you don't care about them, leave them alone until you do. People can sense when you really care. Make sure you check in with them to see how they are doing outside of the church.
4. **Appreciate and respect people, talent, money, and time.** Find creative ways to say thank you.
5. **Check yourself.** What you say, how you say it, what you do, and how you do it send a message. Make sure you are sending the right message.

Frustration with Committee Work

I have never worked on a committee or group project where everybody did a great job and their fair share of the work.

Committee work is that extra thing you end up squeezing into your already busy schedule. You manage to make it to Sunday Worship and midweek services, and now they want to add another meeting time with this committee. They don't meet on time and they stay too late. They spend time discussing other things. Much of what gets accomplished could have been done online or over the phone. For many of us, this sums up our idea of committee work. When this happens, it is very frustrating.

Wisdom ~ Five Tips for Dealing with Frustration with Committee Work

1. **Know what and how much you can handle**. It is better to say no than to say yes and not do it. If you say yes, be clear about what is expected of you.
2. **Committees can be very productive if they have a clear vision** and understanding of their purpose, and cognizant of members' time.
3. **Work in the area of your gifting and talents.**
4. **Expect issues, problems, and challenges.**
5. **Work to maintain a good attitude** while you work.

Conclusion

Someone once compared life in the church to being on Noah's ark. Life must have gotten very inconvenient on the ark with all those animals, but it was a whole lot better than the alternative of drowning

> *And whatsoever ye do, do it heartily, as to the Lord, and not unto men; Knowing that of the Lord ye shall receive the reward of the inheritance: for ye serve the Lord Christ.*
>
> Col 3:23-24

in the flood. There are no perfect congregations. Frustration happens even when you are working for God. Jesus Christ himself had some of the closest people to him lying about him, betraying him, denying him, and doubting him. Yet he pursued and fulfilled his mission and purpose. Always remember Jesus and remember Colossians 3:23-24 KJV. *And whatsoever ye do, do it heartily, as to the Lord, and not unto men; Knowing that of the Lord ye shall receive the reward of the inheritance: for ye serve the Lord Christ.*

PART III

STRATEGIES FOR DEALING WITH FRUSTRATION

PRACTICAL STRATEGIES HELP you deal with frustration. You will be

- Shown how to wait for God
- Encouraged to count your blessings
- Made aware of selective hearing
- Given ways to make good use of frustration
- Reminded to let it go

If followed, these strategies can decrease your level of frustration, help you to avoid frustration, and allow you to experience more peace and joy.

CHAPTER 6

Waiting without Frustration

WAITING . . . DO I really have to? How long is it going take? Can we speed up the process?

My first job was bagging groceries at our local supermarket. That particular supermarket chain has historically been known for good customer service. Every now and then, like during the holidays, we would have a time when the check-out lines were down the grocery aisles. During these times, some customers waited pleasantly until their turn, while others were frustrated and constantly complained. Neither disposition moved the person along faster, but we certainly know who left the store in a better frame of mind.

Yup, people want what they want when they want it; speed is a commodity in our society today. Think of a few of the changes that have been made in recent years. You can have full course meals by microwave in twenty minutes. The US Postal Service is now called "snail mail," because it takes such a "long time" for concrete items to arrive. These days the internet is the way to go for paying bills, shopping, making reservations, and many other things, all at lightning speed. When you do not experience quick, convenient service, you may experience a degree of frustration. In a world of "are we there yets" and "how much longers," do not miss the opportunity of taking the scenic route, stopping to smell the roses, and enjoying the journey.

While fast and convenient is society's preferred method, it is not always the method God chooses. The Bible is full of examples and scriptures exhorting believers to wait for God. Let's review and remember two key persons in the Bible.

God spoke to Abraham, one of my favorite Bible characters, when he was seventy-five years old. God told him to leave his home town and that he, God, would make a great nation from his seed (Gen 12). Abraham left home to go to a place that God would show him as he travelled along the way.

How many people would have started that journey frustrated because they like to know exactly where they are going and the details of how they are going to get there—if they started the journey at all? What about questions like how long is the journey, how many miles are going to be covered daily, what is going to happen when meeting new people and stopping to rest in strange places, and is it going to be safe?

The Bible tells us that Abraham was obedient and went where God told him to go, and after twenty-five years, when Abraham was one hundred years old, God gave him a son, Isaac. Waiting twenty-five years for a promise to be fulfilled can be very frustrating, but Jacob waited for God's time.

Joseph is another of my favorite Bible characters. God gave Joseph a dream. Not just any dream but a vision that God would elevate him. Joseph saw himself in a place of leadership and authority. However, in reality, Joseph found himself in a pit.

God never showed Joseph a dirty, dusty pit in that dream. What happened to Joseph's dreams and plans? This was not the way things were supposed to go, at least not in our human thinking. God did not tell Joseph he would be betrayed by his own brothers and then sold into slavery. Slavery seems to be the exact opposite of being in leadership and authority. Things were getting worse, and it seemed as if Joseph should give up on his dream. However, Joseph kept a good attitude while excelling and exemplifying the utmost integrity as a slave. God never revealed being enslaved to another in Joseph's dreams; yet Joseph experienced being in a place that he did not want to be.

While being a slave of Potiphar, Joseph worked diligently and was a blessing to his master. Potiphar's wife threw herself at Joseph and then lied when Joseph refused to sleep with her. Her dishonesty caused Joseph to end up in prison. Joseph went from a pit to slavery and then to prison. At that point in his life, not only had Joseph not fulfilled his dream, but he had gotten further away from the possibility of reaching it.

As Joseph waited for things in his life to get better, they went from bad to worse to worst. Joseph spent over two years in prison until finally one day God fulfilled the vision he had given Joseph. In just one day, Joseph became second in command in all of Egypt when he interpreted the Pharaoh's dream.

Joseph remained faithful to God through every disappointing and distressing moment of his life. It seemed as though God had forgotten about Joseph; however, the Bible declared that God was with Joseph in all of his circumstances. Each bad thing brought Joseph one step closer to the fulfillment of God's promise. God made Joseph's latter days more than compensate him for the struggles of his past. Joseph did not simply wait. He blessed others and learned a great deal. Like Joseph, you should not waste your wait time. Use that time wisely.

Some things in life, both big and small, are worth the wait. For example, at a theme park our little group waited in line for an hour for a three-minute ride on a roller coaster. Those three minutes were so worth the wait that we got in line to do it all over again. Sometimes what God has in store for us is so good and so great that it is worth waiting for what we consider a long time.

It is helpful to know you don't have to wait alone. God will be with you every step of the way. Have you ever been on a road trip where you had a good conversation with someone in the car, played games, or sang songs, instead of focusing on every mile? You were at your destination much more quickly than you anticipated because you didn't wait alone— and you chose to enjoy the journey. In your Christian journey if you focus on the fact that you have great company that you can enjoy while you wait, waiting will become much easier, much less frustrating, and much more pleasant. Adjust your attitude about waiting from simply enduring it to enjoying the many other people and things that fill your world. It will make a huge difference in the quality of your life.

Patience has more to do with your attitude while you wait than actually waiting. It is important that you realize that everything God promised will come to pass. God is omnipotent and omniscient; therefore he is not bound by time. Being human, you are bound by time and seasons. You must realize that your times are in God's hand.

Job said it best when he said, *All the days of my appointed time will I wait, until my change come.* Job 14:14 KJV. Job understood there are appointed times for things to happen in life. If you wait, a change will come. When you have ultimate trust that God will fulfill his promise, you can rest assured and be confident that God is faithful and capable of doing everything HE said. A deferment does not mean you are denied. Consider the following things while you wait:

- God knows the best way to do things.
- Sometimes when you are being hasty, things are done the wrong way.
- God knows the best time to do things.
- Timing can make or break a great opportunity.
- Enjoy the journey.

Make sure you are not the hold-up. It is true that while you think you are waiting for God, God is actually waiting for you. Perhaps God has been telling you to do things that will prepare you for the blessing he has in store for you. Obedience is essential to receive the promises of God. You must also do your part to be fully prepared to obtain your desire. The person who is waiting for God to bless him or her with a job should update the resume and practice some interviewing techniques. Then when God provides an opportunity for an interview, the person is ready.

Finally take your eyes off the clock and enjoy the scenery. Think about traveling with a clock watcher. That person who is always asking, "Are we there yet?" or "How much longer?" Time is much better spent enjoying what is being seen and heard. This earthly life really is a journey, and God wants you to enjoy the journey rather than being overwhelmed with frustration.

Conclusion

> The healthier, better, and wiser choice is to wait with peace and joy while enjoying the journey.

Yes we do have to wait sometimes in life. Yes waiting can be uncertain, uncomfortable, and undesirable. Whether you are frustrated, angry, and irritable or calm, peaceful, and joyous; you still have to wait. The healthier, better, and wiser choice is to wait with peace and joy while enjoying the journey.

CHAPTER 7

Remembering How and What to Count

I CAN REMEMBER a turning point early in my marriage. Now, I am blessed with a very good memory. One not-so-good thing about it was that I was remembering everything unfavorable that my wife did or said. I could tell her when she said it and the circumstances surrounding what she said.

One day we were studying the Bible together and we read 1 Corinthians 13 in a different translation from what I had read before. As we read that *love keeps no record of wrongs,* my wife looked at me, and I knew I was guilty. After that Bible study I began praying and asking God to help me not count and keep record when others do or say things that I don't appreciate. Please note: This does mean that people who repeatedly do wrong and do not correct the wrongdoings should not be held accountable. They, too, become people to stay away from.

Some people make an extensive list of everything that is going wrong or problematic in their lives. If they are not careful, they find themselves complaining to anyone who will listen. Instead of being

> As Christians, we are the light of the world. We can't afford to have our light diminished by the gloom and darkness of others.

someone who others can come to for a word of encouragement, they become labeled as the person to avoid. Have you ever been feeling great and asked someone how they were doing? Then, by the time they finished complaining about everything, you notice that the wonderful feeling you had was no longer there? As Christians, we are the light of the world. We can't afford to have our light diminished by the gloom and darkness of others.

What would happen if every day you made a diligent effort to count your blessings?

Hymns are biblical concepts put to music. Johnson Oatman Jr. wrote a popular hymn that makes this point:

Chorus
Count your blessings, name them one by one.
Count your blessings, see what God hath done.
Count your blessings, name them one by one.
Count your many blessings, see what God hath done.

Bing Crosby later recorded "When I get worried and I can't sleep, I count my blessings instead of sheep. And I fall asleep counting my blessings."

If you are going to count, why not count your blessings? I guarantee you will find them too numerous to count. But try.

How many times has God . . .

Taken care of you when you did something careless?

Remember the time when you could have been hurt badly or even killed because you were acting foolishly or just not thinking or paying attention.

Helped you through a rough situation?

What about the time you lost a love one, a source of income, a great opportunity? Think about the roughest and toughest times you have ever had in your life. God was there and HE helped you get through it. Illness, financial difficulty, depression—and the list goes on and on. If you have ever experienced any of these things, God was there and He brought you through them.

Believers are not exempt from hurt, pain, disappointment, turmoil, or trouble. In fact Jesus declared that you would have it and that you are blessed when you suffer. I have had situations where I am simply amazed at the power of God when I look back at what he brought me through and how he kept me and worked everything out for my good. There were times when my knowledge and my resources could not help me in any way. God stepped in and showed himself strong. If you think about it, you will see that he has done the same for you.

Given you something good you did not deserve?

Every believer can relate to being granted something worldly he or she did not deserve. Remember also that it is truly by grace that people are saved. When you allow yourself to reflect on your deliverance, freedom, and inheritance, it becomes evident that you are blessed and highly favored.

Withheld something bad you did deserve?

Think about the concept of justification. One of the greatest blessings given to everyone who will receive it is justification. Although you may be guilty of something (or many things), God makes it just as if you never sinned at all.

When my cousin was murdered, I was leaving my aunt and called my wife to inform her of the funeral plans, when suddenly there were lights behind me, and I was being pulled over. The last thing I needed was a ticket, and I truly did not know how fast I was driving. My heart began beating faster and I began feeling nauseous. The state trooper asked for my license and registration and went back to his car. He returned with my license, registration, and another piece of paper, and told me to be careful. I looked at the paper expecting it to be a ticket only to find that it was a warning. I was so grateful, and I thanked God all the way back to my destination, and of course I slowed down. God had given me the warning by way of the trooper.

I really deserved a ticket. I really could not afford a ticket. I was blessed to receive only a warning instead of suffering something much worse than a ticket. Think of the times this has happened to you. There were times when you should have been punished or given severe consequences, but you were given mercy. You were given another chance. When you are the recipient of God's mercy, pay attention, thank God, and learn the lesson that God has put before you.

There is much to learn from studying the life of David. He was anointed and designated to be king of Israel at a young age. He was a successful warrior and giant slayer, but he had some major mess ups and bad decisions in his life. He had the prior king out to kill him, causing him to live life on the run and hiding from place to place. He had family issues with his children, including death right after birth, rape, and murder. It is safe to say David had more than his share of trouble throughout his life. But look at David's attitude as expressed in Psalms. David was always praising and thanking God.

In Psalm 103:2 NLT, David wrote, *Let all that I am praise the LORD; may I never forget the good things he does for me.* David spent the rest of Psalm 103 talking about the good things or the benefits God gave him. The list of benefits from God included but was not limited to redemption, forgiveness, compassion, mercy, and love. Instead of making a list of all his problems, David chose to list the good things God did for him. Like David, you should endeavor to spend more time counting your blessings instead of counting your problems.

Conclusion

The truth of the matter is that God has always been good, and God still is good. He looks after you and cares for you in innumerable ways every day.

> The truth of the matter is that God has always been good, and God still is good.

How far can you count? What is the highest number? Whether it is a million, billion, or trillion, no matter how massive the number, you have enough blessings to cover that number. Start your list today.

CHAPTER 8

Getting the Proverbial Hearing Aid and Using It

I HAVE BEEN fortunate to have some great aunts. One among them is Aunt Mamie. Aunt Mamie is very sweet, but a little hard of hearing. Aunt Mamie has the tendency to not wear her hearing aid or to turn it down so she does not hear a lot of background noise. When this happens, Aunt Mamie looks at the person talking, smiles, and nods her head to everything that is being said. She has mastered this technique to the point that you really have to know her or be saying something horrible to know that she does not really hear you. If someone walked up to me and said I was rude and ignorant, it would cause me some level of stress. If someone walked up to Aunt Mamie, when her hearing aid was turned down and said the same thing, she would simply smile and go about her day with no stress at all.

Consider this: What is the quality or importance of what Aunt Mamie is missing out on because she does not turn her hearing aid up? Those who really know her make sure that she hears and understands the pertinent information. For those she really knows, she makes a special effort to hear and understand what they are saying. Aunt Mamie has chosen to listen to what matters in life and to tune out the rest. Likewise, get yourself an internal hearing aid and choose when to focus your attention on hearing—and not hearing—certain things from certain people. This does not mean to ignore things you just don't like; it does mean to ignore what is not important and what does not improve life.

Let's take a closer look at some principles behind the metaphorical hearing aid.

Know when to turn your hearing aid down and smile.

How many times have you become upset, irritated, uneasy, and frustrated because someone who was angry, bitter, and also frustrated said something negative and unnecessary? Whether it was a family member, a church member, or a customer or client at work, it affected the rest of your day. Yes, there are some times when you need to turn up your hearing aid and really listen to what is being said and do something about it. However, there are times when you receive misdirected anger from someone who is just a complainer, or someone is acting out of jealousy, fear, and/or ignorance. Then it's time to turn your hearing aid down.

I have taught courses in higher education for the past seven years. In the early semesters when I received the teacher evaluation forms, the comments were generally good and above the average score for the department. In addition to that, there were some absolutely great comments. Yet, there were still a few negative comments. It would literally take me days and sometimes weeks to get past those comments. I would forget about the overall wonderful score and the additional great comments to focus on the negative comments. I took them as fact, instead of as just one person's opinion.

You must learn the difference between fact and opinion. Make sure that you listen to and address the facts. Be selective about the opinions you listen to, and be careful about

> Be selective about the opinions you listen to, and be careful about how much credence and power you give them in your life.

how much credence and power you give them in your life. In my case, I worried and beat myself up about a few students' opinions. These were most likely the students who failed and poorly attended the class. It was not my direct supervisor, not my well trained colleagues, but a minority of students who did not master the subject that I allowed to get me down. Don't let this kind of thing happen to you.

Remember this: negative people are everywhere. It is important not to let them and their negativity sabotage your thinking and rob you of your motivation. These are the individuals for whom you purposely turn your hearing aid down when in their presence. Their comments are unhelpful, depressing, pessimistic, and destructive.

One rule of thumb: Before you get frustrated, consider the source. The problem may not be yours, but the other person's.

DR. ADRIAN MANLEY

Some things you are better off not knowing

Many years ago I did not believe that I was better off not knowing some things. I thought I needed to know everything people thought, felt, and did that had any relation to me or the people I love. Life has a way of teaching many lessons. One day I heard something that I could not shake. It consumed my thoughts and energy for weeks. I just could not believe what I had heard about a certain person. How could it be? Why would the person do such a thing? I asked myself many questions and I even attempted to answer some of those questions. Obviously what I heard caused me some degree of disappointment and sorrow. However, the information had no bearing on me, or my loved ones. There are some things in life that I have no need of knowing and am better off not knowing.

The lesson is this: know when to stop a person and say, "Please tell me this information only if it has an impact on me or someone I care about." Think about something that was shared with you that you would have been much happier and less stressed not knowing. There are times when it is not in your best interest to know. The next time someone comes to you to tell you something negative, ask the following three questions:

1. Ask the person if the information has an impact on you or someone you care about. If the answer is that it does, listen carefully.
2. Ask yourself what is the best thing you should do with this information. Be honest with yourself about it. There are some things you may not want to know, but you need know.
3. If the information doesn't have an impact on you or someone you care about, ask the person not to tell you any more.

One example of the three-step process was my first experience with a hurricane in central Florida. I remember being so nervous that I could not sleep. I stayed glued to the TV and radio so that I could constantly hear everything that was going on with the hurricane. My wife, who is from south Florida and experienced hurricane Andrew, finally said, "Adrian, turn off the TV and radio. They are only stressing you out."

Did I need to know there was hurricane? Yes, and I was prepared. Did I need to stay glued to the TV and radio hearing all the details? No. In fact after I turned off the TV and radio, I started to settle down, rest, and enjoy the quiet time.

Conclusion

Remember that words truly are powerful and they impact people, including you, for a long time. You can probably remember negative things said to you many years ago. Knowing the difference between what you do not need to hear and what you absolutely need to hear even though it is hard to face hugely impacts the quality of your life. Use this chapter to help you decide, when the time comes, what is really important to know. Choose wisely.

> When the time comes, what is really important to know? Choose wisely.

CHAPTER 9

Using Frustration and Letting It Go

I S FRUSTRATION ALWAYS a bad thing? Can something good come out of frustration?

Frustration is not always a bad thing. If you pay attention to it, something good can indeed come out of frustration.

Yes, it is worth revisiting the old adage "take lemons and make lemonade." You can benefit from frustration if you learn how to use it and then to let it go. First, you can let frustration motivate you to make things right. In addition, you can let the frustration you experience teach you how to avoid it in the future. Frustration can be a great agent of change, if only you will let it. Therefore, frustration can be beneficial if you use it for motivation or for learning a valuable lesson.

Transforming Frustration into Motivation

> Frustration can be beneficial if you use it for motivation or for learning a valuable lesson.

As a therapist, I pay attention to the processes people use to make changes in their lives. One major issue is women who leave abusive relationships after a long period of time. For several years women suffer degradation, manipulation, and harm. They deal with severe abuse and mistreatment for various reasons. Some of those reasons are fear, lack of finances, no place to go, hope that things will change, trying to help the abuser, and not wanting to be alone.

So what makes these women finally leave? Here are some of the factors they have reported to me: I saw the effect on my children, I almost died, I just got sick and tired, I got tired of being sick and tired, I couldn't take it anymore, I realized that unless I did something things would stay the same or get worse. In other words, the circumstances provided the motivation to change.

Why constantly live in a state of frustration—or fear—when you can do something about your frustrating—or dangerous—situation? Use the frustration in your life to motivate you to change.

Are you frustrated about the fact that you can't fit into all those nice clothes in your closet? Use that frustration as motivation to start an exercise regime or change some of your eating habits. Are you frustrated that some of your family relationships are strained? Use that frustration to create a realistic plan for dealing with those family members. Are you frustrated about where you are in your career or how you are being treated on your job? Use that frustration as motivation to get the training or the education to get a better job and move forward in your career. Are you frustrated about the way things are going in your church? Use that frustration as motivation to be a change agent, and start a prayer group, have conversation with your church leadership, or find out how you can be a part of the solution.

In 2 Kings 7, the Bible records the story of four men with leprosy sitting at the entrance of the city gate of an enemy's camp. The men were hungry, frustrated, and scared. Finally, they began to ask themselves if it made sense to just sit at the same spot in the same situation and die. After weighing their options they decided they were not going to sit there and die; they were going into the enemy's camp. To their surprise, no enemies were there. God had caused the enemies to hear the clatter of speeding chariots and armies, and the enemies had fled.

These four leprous men who decided to do something about their frustrating situation found themselves in a camp full of food, silver, and gold. As you think of this story, I encourage you to use your frustration as motivation to get up and do something. The four men could have easily continued sitting outside the city gate, moping and frustrated at their situation. They could have chosen to sit there and die. But these four leprous men got up and took action to end their frustrating situation. You can do the same.

Whatever the area and source of your frustrations, follow The 5 Steps for Frustration Transformation:

1. **Identify the source of your frustration**. Honestly assess the root cause of your frustration.

DR. ADRIAN MANLEY

2. **Take responsibility for your role in your frustration.**
3. **Decide what you can change** and make one long-term goal and three short-term goals that are Specific, Measurable, Achievable, Realistic, and Time Sensitive. (SMART goals are criteria set by business psychologist George Doran.) Remember: a goal is a dream with timeframe.
4. **Create a weekly plan** for achieving your goals and a weekly progress monitoring form to keep track of and evaluate your progress (see forms in the appendices). Pay special attention to your level of frustration as you work your plan.
5. **Take time every week to evaluate the week** and make a new plan for the upcoming week based on your goals. Celebrate your successes and work on your shortcomings. Continue this process until you have reached your long-term goal.

Example of Frustration Transformation

1. **Source of Frustration**—I have a lack of finances and am living paycheck to paycheck.
2. **My responsibility**—I should reverse my current situation of having poor spending habits, no savings, and no budget.
3. **My Long-term Goal**—By the end of the year I will not be living paycheck to paycheck. I will have saved the equivalent of two paychecks. (This goal is Specific, Measurable, Achievable, Realistic, and Time Sensitive.)

   My Short-term Goals—I will create a budget, start a savings account that I contribute to monthly, and change problematic spending habits.

   Plan for week one—I will start creating a budget. I will list all bills and monthly expenses, list monthly income, and determine where I waste money or spend frivolously. I will talk to my employer about possibilities for overtime.

   Plan for week two—I will create a formal budget with and allotment for savings.

   Plan for week four—I will evaluate the budget, make changes if need be. I will look for more ways of being more efficient with my money (maybe cooking more and taking lunches instead of eating out so much).

Use Frustration to teach you the lesson not to get into similar frustrating situations.

How many times do you have to fall into the same hole before you realize it's there? How many times do you have to be burned by the same box of matches before you start using a lighter (whether we're talking about something concrete like starting the fire in a grill or some of the more abstract situations in life)? Some people learn quickly from their mistakes and the mistakes of others. Some people learn only the hard way by making the same mistakes repeatedly or following the same path that caused problems for others. It is my hope that you will be able to look at some frustrations in your life and determine that this is the last time you will experience them.

A college student came to me with high level of frustration about her relationship with her boyfriend. She was giving her all to the relationship. She cooked, cleaned, paid bills, and supported his goals and dreams. She helped him get a job and helped him with his homework. She was frustrated because he did not spend much time with her or pay a lot of attention to her.

I asked her, "What does he do for you?" She paused for a long time and replied, "He keeps me from being alone." Being the counselor that I am, I challenged her by saying, "So your issue is that the person who keeps you from being alone is not paying attention to you and not spending time with you."

That's when it happened. She asked, "Why can't men appreciate a good woman? I have been in three relationships in the past two years and I know that I am a good woman. I treated each one of these guys like they were kings. I put them first and did all I could to help them. I never ask for a lot. Just love me and spend some time with me. I am not one of those high maintenance women."

You can probably see some of the issues around her frustration. She seemed to be picking the same type of guy and being the same type of woman and wondering why she was having the same type of frustration. We addressed her issues of self-esteem, fear of loneliness, and working to buy or earn someone's love. At the end of our work together, she became aware of why and how she kept inviting the same kind of frustration into her life, and she broke the cycle.

Perhaps your situation is different from a relationship issue. Whatever the issue is that frustrates you, it can teach you a lesson. You must learn how to learn from every experience in life, especially the frustrating and bad experiences. There is an old adage that says, "First time shame on you, second time shame on me." The adage implies that people should learn their lessons the first time. Although you may not get it right the first or second time, you should endeavor to stop repeating the same mistakes and causing yourself the same frustrations over and over again.

> You must learn how to learn from every experience in life, especially the frustrating and bad experiences.

Conclusion

Take a look at the frustration in your life. Before you get rid of it, see what you can get out of it. Transform that frustration into motivation for elevation. Use it to help you rise. Use it as the weight to build your muscle and make you stronger. Use the experience to make you smarter and wiser. When you have used your frustration to the fullest, kick it out of your life and let it go.

> Transform that frustration into motivation for elevation.

PART IV

FINAL WORDS OF WISDOM TO DEAL WITH FRUSTRATION

F RUSTRATION IS A normal emotional state resulting from not achieving a goal or something desired, or from feeling deprived of someone or something desired, gratifying, needed, and/or deserved.

- Everyone must deal with frustration in life.
- Whether it involves family, friends, workplace, or church, frustration happens.
- No one has to live in a state of constant frustration, especially the believer.

Frustrated people tend to be disgruntled, stressed, irritated, annoyed, and less productive. God does not want you to spend your life feeling that way. Although you do not have the power to control or stop certain things from happening, you do have the power to control your attitude and response to anything that will happen in your life. The Bible gives you several ways of dealing with your challenges. Instead of remaining in a state of frustration, consistently practice the following principles from the Word of God.

Jesus said in John 14:27 NLT, *I am leaving you with a gift—peace* (*eirene* in Greek) *of mind and heart, And the peace I give is a gift the world cannot give.* Peace in the context of this scripture signifies contentment, security, tranquility, and freedom from inward turmoil. This peace is the inheritance of every believer. Jesus left it for you. After dealing with all the challenges he dealt with, HE knew that you would need peace.

Think of all the things Jesus had to deal with in his life and ministry. Even before his death, he was constantly lied about and talked about. Jesus was consistently called into question about the good that he was doing, people doubted his identity and his ability, and they refused to give him the honor and recognition that was due him. He was despised, rejected, hated, and misunderstood. All of this happened before he was degraded, tortured, and persecuted like a criminal.

Jesus further instructed you, the believer, in that verse not to let your heart be troubled (*tarassō* in Greek). Being troubled in the context of this verse means being anxious, or distressed. GOD is the most trustworthy being in the world. We can totally and completely trust him. When we reach the point of absolute trust and confidence in God, we will experience less frustration. I am reminded of the lyrics written by Elisha A. Hoffman in the hymn "Leaning on the Everlasting Arms":

What a fellowship, what a joy divine
Leaning on the everlasting arms.
What a blessedness, what a peace is mine,
Leaning on the everlasting arms.

What have I to dread, what have I to fear,
Leaning on the everlasting arms;
I have blessed peace with my Lord so near,
Leaning on the everlasting arms.

> When we reach the point of absolute trust and confidence in God, we will experience less frustration.

Jesus left his peace, his security, rest, and tranquility for you. Jesus knows about every struggle you will ever go through, and every time the devil will endeavor to keep you stressed, discouraged, and frustrated. HE did not promise that you would not have troubles, but He did leave us HIS peace to ensure that you can go through them all without overwhelming distress and frustration. We have no need continue to be troubled or disturbed by anything. This is not to say things will not be troublesome or burdensome. In fact the opposite is true. In life we will experience many unfavorable circumstances and situations. But when we have the Holy Spirit, we have an internal thermostat that will keep us cool on the inside as we go through the fire.

In Matthew 11:28, Jesus extended a wonderful opportunity for all those who labor and are heavy laden to come to him and learn of him. Jesus promised those laborers and heavy laden persons rest. Labor (*kopiaō* in Greek) in this context means to grow weary, tired, exhausted from toil or burdens or grief. Heavy laden (*phortizō* in Greek) in this context means greatly burdened or loaded up with something. Rest (*anapauō* in the Greek) in this context means a state of quietness, calmness, recovery, and patient expectation.

How many times have you grown weary dealing with the multiple ups and downs and challenges of life? Even now, there are likely some unfavorable things going on in your life. Furthermore, you did not ask for nor do you feel you deserve these things. Yes, it's true: Life happens to everyone and life is not fair. As a believer you must remember your standing invitation from Jesus, and his promise to give you rest. Have you ever been to the point where you just need a break? Jesus promises that you can find that break and even more in him. In fact, He will give you quietness and calmness, and refresh you right in the midst of the storms in your life. You must constantly lay claim on and walk in the "rest" that Jesus promises you.

Finally, remember and practice three verses the Apostle Paul wrote when dealing with frustration. Paul writes in 1 Thessalonians 5:16-18 NLT, *Always be joyful. Never stop praying. Be thankful in all circumstances, for this is God's will for you who belong to Christ Jesus.*

Find something to be joyful about, and do it. There is so much to pray about; do it. Certainly you are blessed with a great deal to be thankful about; do it. The person who is consistently and constantly joyful, praying, and thankful will not live in a state of frustration.

It is my hope that you use the word of God to effectively deal with the frustration in your life, so that you can spend your time living, loving, helping, and enjoying the many blessings God has given you.

> Use the word of God to effectively deal with the frustration in your life, so that you can spend your time living, loving, helping, and enjoying the many blessings God has given you.

APPENDICES

5 Steps for Frustration Transformation Form

1. **What is the source of my frustration?**

   _____

   _____

2. **What is my responsibility in this frustrating situation?**

   _____

   _____

3. **What are my one long-term goal and two short goals for change?**
   (This goal is Specific, Measurable, Achievable, Realistic, and Time Sensitive.)

   _____

   _____

4. **What is my plan for achieving these goals this week?**

   _____

   _____

5. **What is my evaluation for the week and how can I do better next week?**

   _____

   _____

Weekly Goal Setting Exercise

1. Write one goal you would like to achieve this week. Be specific.

_____

_____

_____

_____

_____

2. What is your plan this week for achieving your goal?

_____

_____

_____

_____

_____

3. What is going to be your biggest challenge in accomplishing your plan?

_____

_____

_____

_____

_____

4. How are you going to overcome this challenge?

_____

_____

_____

_____

_____

5. How will you know if you you succeeded this week?

_____

_____

_____

_____

_____

Weekly Progress Monitoring Form

(Photocopy and fill in. Repeat as needed)

Galatians 6:4 NLT: *Pay careful attention to your own work, for then you will get the satisfaction of a job well done, and you won't need to compare yourself to anyone else.*

1. What was your goal for this week? Be specific.

_____

_____

_____

_____

_____

2. What was your plan this week for achieving your goal?

_____

_____

_____

_____

_____

3. What was your biggest challenge in accomplishing your plan?

_____

_____

_____

_____

_____

4. What insights or noteable moments did you have this week?

_____

_____

_____

_____

_____

5. On a scale of 1 (Low) to 5 (High), rate your success in completing your plan and tell why.

_____

_____

_____

_____

_____

_____

6. On a scale of 1 (Low) to 5 (High), grade yourself on your effort this week. Why?

_____

_____

_____

_____

_____

7. What did you do well?

_____

_____

_____

_____

_____

8. What could you have done better?

_____

_____

_____

_____

_____